TOGETHER

A First Book About Race for Awesome Kids

Written by Shayla Reese Griffin
Illustrated by Christina O.

Justice Leaders ◉ PRESS
Detroit, MI

Awesome kids of every race live

together

in the United States.

But it wasn't always this way...

A long, long, long time ago all people lived **together** in Africa

Then we started moving!

And even though we were still the same on the inside, we started to think of each other as different **races**.

Did You Know?

Humans have different skin colors because of how our bodies adapted to different amounts of sunlight in different parts of the world.

Our race is mostly based
on the place our
ancestors—our
grandparents',
grandparents',
grandparents',
grandparents',
grandparents'
grandparents—
lived.

People whose ancestors
stayed in Africa the longest are

Black.

Fun Fact!
The Dogon people of Mali
were some of the world's
first astronomers!

People whose ancestors
were the first to live in
North and South America are
Indigenous or **Native**
American.

People whose ancestors

lived in Asia are

Asian.

Fun Fact!
People from China invented the first fireworks in the world!

People whose ancestors

lived on islands in the Pacific Ocean are

Pacific Islander.

Did You Know?
Pacific Islanders were some of the first people on the planet to cross oceans!

People whose ancestors

lived in Europe are

White.

People whose ancestors

lived in southwest Asia or north Africa are

Middle Eastern or **North African**

(MENA).

People who are more

than one race are

Multiracial or **Biracial.**

Did You Know?
Multiracial people sometimes use the term Mixed to describe themselves, or they may name their specific racial identities. Some identify with only one of their racial groups.

Fun Fact
Most of us are probably a little bit of a mix because each one of us has thousands of ancestors and there's a good chance they came from different places.

And people whose ancestors lived in Mexico, Central America, South America, or some Caribbean Islands are **Latine, Latinx,** or **Latino.**

Our awesome ancestors
moved all around the
world.

They walked!
They rode on
boats and trains!
They flew in airplanes!

And now in the United States, awesome kids of every race live **together**.

Shayla Reese Griffin, PhD, MSW is co-founder of Justice Leaders Collaborative, an organization committed to dismantling oppression, cultivating justice, and nurturing wellbeing through social justice training, consulting, books, and resources. Shayla is the author of *The Awesome Kids Guide to Race*, *Those Kids, Our Schools: Race and Reform in An American High School*, and co-author of *Race Dialogues: A Facilitator's Guide to Tackling the Elephant in the Classroom*. She is Black American and has an interracial family that includes people who are Black, White, Indigenous, Multiracial, and Latina. She lives with her spouse and three children and gets her best ideas at 3 am.

Christina O. is a multidisciplinary artist who specializes in fine art, puppetry, wood burning, jewelry design, and illustration. She utilizes a variety of textures and materials along with more traditional mediums. Her art draws inspiration from her Afro-Latina roots, motherhood, the loved ones around her, social and political events, her travels abroad, and moments of self reflection. Christina O. has had her work printed on the pages of Pikchur magazine, has been commissioned by Black Lives Matter, is a member of the international art society Kappa Pi, and has shown her work in various galleries on the East Coast. Her goal for the work she creates is that it will exude the depths of the human spirit and the rhythm of life.

Justice Leaders 🔥 PRESS

Published in 2025 in Detroit, MI by Justice Leaders Press www.justiceleaderspress.com
Text Copyright @ 2025 Shayla Reese Griffin
Illustrations Copyright @ 2025 Christina O.
Book Design by Tori Griffin & Shayla Reese Griffin
Edited by David Dobbie
Contributions by Victoria L. Birch and Margarette Griffin

Paperback ISBN: 979-8-9886449-2-7
Hardcover ISBN: 979-8-9886449-3-4
Library of Congress Control Number: 2024909931

If you enjoyed this book and want more from
Justice Leaders Press
please consider supporting our work!

· ·

☐ 1. Leave a great review on the site where you purchased this book!

☐ 2. Ask your local library or bookstore to carry *Together: A First Book About Race for Awesome Kids.*

☐ 3. Share our book with someone in your life!

☐ 4. Place a bulk order on our website for your school or organization!

Visit **www.JusticeLeadersPress.com** for more resources on how to talk to kids about race, merch, and free downloads.